SUPERHERO COFFEE BEANS!

STORIES FROM IN2ED AFRICA

BOOK 8

EMMA DREDGE

ACKNOWLEDGMENTS

Thank you to the amazing children of Korogocho slums in Kenya who have inspired this book.

And thank YOU for buying a copy of Superhero Coffee Beans! All money raised from the profits of this book will ensure that the children in Korogocho can continue their education and reach their own potential. As part of our books4books program your purchase will go towards providing the same book to a child in Korogocho. This will be used to promote a love of books, develop literacy skills and enable them to build up their own home library.

Thank you too to Trade, Development & The Environment Hub who were the source of information about the coffee making process, from the seed to the cup.

For Tashania, a real life superhero.

"Dad, how do we get coffee?" asked 9 year old Ted.

Ted was in a cafe with his Dad. He watched the waiters bustling around carrying delicious looking food to different tables.

Dad put his newspaper down and leant forwards. "It takes a lot of hard work Ted. We need...

Mother sun to shine her rays.
	Water from some rainy days.
	Farmers and their skillful ways
	That's how coffee's made."

"But Dad, what I mean is...."

"... you want to know how it all comes together?" Dad interrupted.

He whispered something to a passing waiter. The waiter returned holding what looked like a small brown pebble. He gave it to Dad.

"What's that?" asked Ted.

"This" said Dad holding the pebble-like thing between his thumb and finger, "is a coffee bean. And it is more valuable than gold."

Ted scoffed. "More valuable than gold? I don't believe it."

"It's true" cried Dad, jumping up from his chair. "Each of these little coffee beans has incredible, extraordinary, super-sonic powers."

Ted leant back in his chair and folded his arms. "Really? Can they fly? Can they turn back time?"

"They can do MUCH better things than that" squealed Dad.

And he sang...
> *"Coffee beans are tough, made of special stuff*
> *Superheroes, beans of might*
> *Amazing, awesome, they're alright!"*

Ted rolled his eyes. "Superheroes? Are you serious?"

"Of course!" laughed Dad. "These little coffee beans have more powers than you could possibly imagine."

"Like what?" Ted folded his arms and stared at Dad.

Dad beckoned for Ted to come closer. Then he whispered in his ear "They are shape shifters."

"You mean they can actually change their shape?" asked Ted. "Nonsense!"

"It's all absolutely true I tell you" whooped Dad. "It all starts with a white flower - a pretty, beautiful, wonderful smelling flower. But these flowers don't hang around for long! After a few days, they wither away and coffee cherries appear. It takes up to 14 months for the cherries to ripen. The farmers know when they are fully ripe, because the cherries turn red.

Then the cherries are picked.

"So what?" said Ted. "What's the big deal?"

"What's the big deal? I'll tell you what the big deal is. It means that they can change their colour, shape and size. What started off as a tree, turned into a white flower, THEN into red cherries, THEN into these amazing coffee beans. Now that is a superpower."

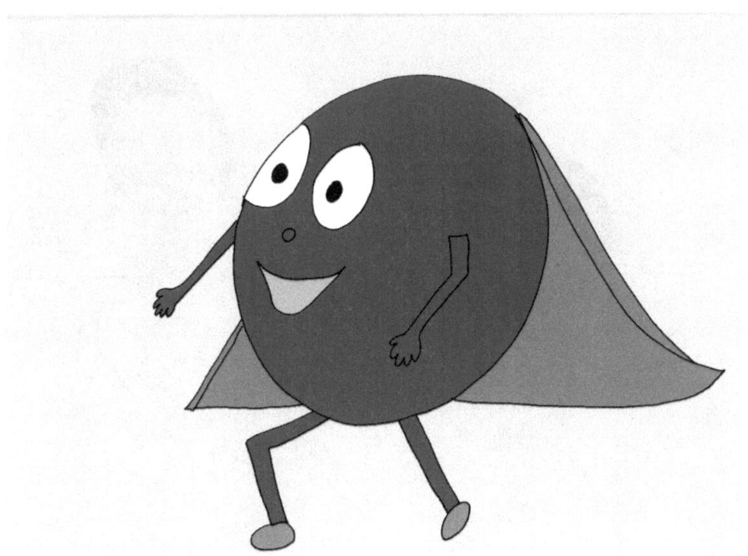

And he sang...

> *"Coffee beans are tough, made of special*
> *stuff*
> *Changing shape and size, right before*
> *our eyes*
> *Superheroes, beans of might*
> *Amazing, awesome, they're alright!"*

Ted played with the handle of his coffee cup. "But Dad, what I *really* want to know is...."

"Yes, you want to know what happens next" said Dad. "OK, let me tell you.

Once the cherries have all been picked, it is time to start processing. (This means to change something using a special treatment). The coffee beans need to be removed from the cherries. This is done by spreading the cherries in the sun until they are all dried out and turn green. Only the ripest and best beans are chosen!"

Dad stood up from his chair and ran to the other side of the table. He grabbed Ted's shoulders excitedly and said, "You know what that means? It means they have another superpower – the power to brave the heat of the sun!"

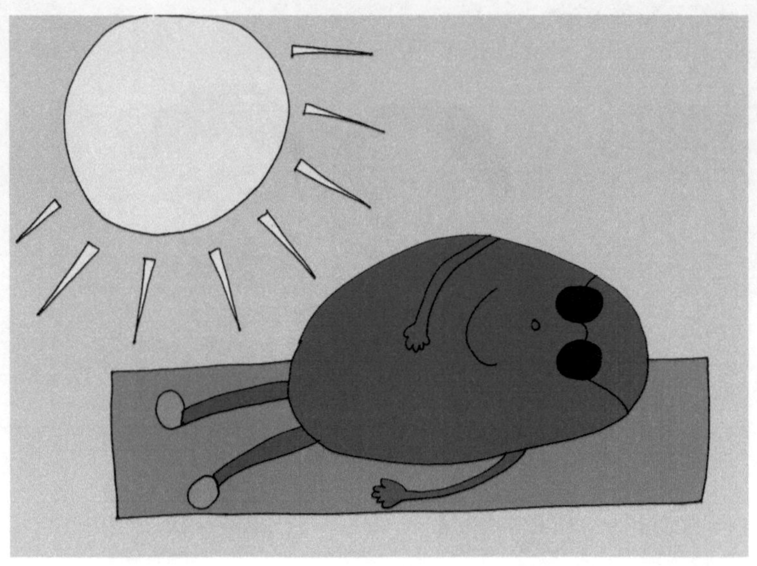

And he sang...

> *"Coffee beans are tough, made of special*
>   *stuff*
> *Changing shape and size, right before*
>   *our eyes*
> *Drying in the sun, baking till they're done*
>
> *Superheroes, beans of might*
> *Amazing, awesome, they're alright!"*

Ted sighed. He was getting tired of all this. "Dad, please listen. Can't you just tell me...."

"What happens next? Of course I can my boy!" Dad leapt over to his side of the table again, knocking over a chair as he went. "The next stage is very exciting.

The beans are roasted to get their special flavour and aroma (that means smell). It is quite a skill to get this right and usually takes between 7 – 14 minutes. As the roasting goes on, the beans turn a scrumptious brown colour and actually POP, just like corn!

Imagine being roasted until going pop? Humans could never cope with that. But coffee beans can! Oh yes, they have super-powers of incredible strength."

Dad flexed his biceps to show the strength of the coffee beans and Ted giggled at the sight of his Dad's stick-like arm.

And Dad sang...

> *"Coffee beans are tough, made of special*
>   *stuff*
> *Changing shape and size, right before*
>   *our eyes*
> *Drying in the sun, baking till they're done*
> *Roasting all the beans, using big machines*
>
> *Superheroes, beans of might*
> *Amazing, awesome, they're alright!"*

Ted rested his chin in his hands. "Dad, that's pretty cool, but really all I want to know is...."

But Dad wasn't listening. He was talking to a waiter who handed him a glass jar.

"What's that?" asked Ted.

Dad opened the lid of the glass jar.

"Ahhh, smell that Ted" he said. "Just stick your nose inside and take a great big sniff."

Ted did as he was told and instantly his nostrils were filled with the aroma of coffee. He had to admit it smelt pretty good.

"But this is a brown powder" he said. "Where are the coffee beans?"

"Aha!" Dad bellowed. "These are they... I mean this is them... I mean, these are the coffee beans!

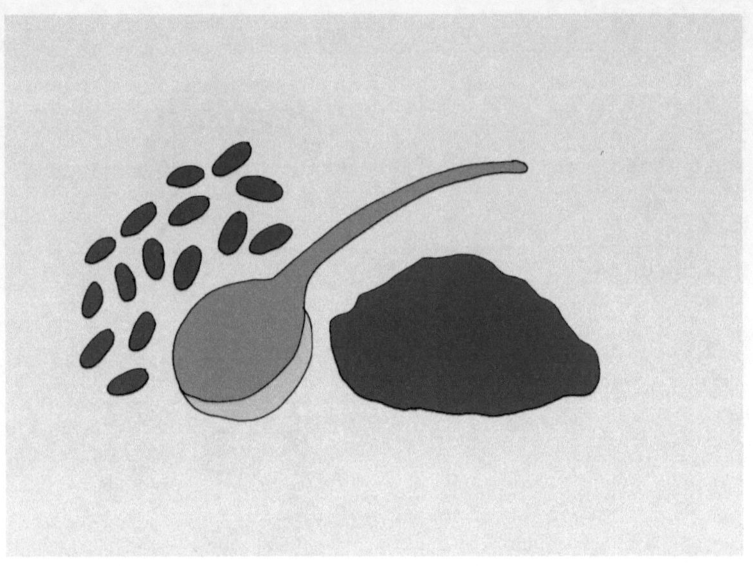

We grind the beans down into a fine powder so that the coffee can be made into the delicious, scrumptious drink that it is. That's called brewing.

Which leads me on to another superhero power that coffee beans have. The power to boost our moods. Just the smelling of freshly ground coffee makes people feel good.

And Dad sang...

> *Coffee beans are tough, made of special stuff*
> *Changing shape and size, right before*
> *   our eyes*
> *Drying in the sun, baking till they're done*
> *Roasting all the beans, using big machines*
> *Now we grind and brew, that's the thing*
> *   to do*
>
> *Superheroes, beans of might*
> *Amazing, awesome, they're alright!"*

By this time, a group of new customers had walked in and were watching Dad in amazement.

They were staring.

They were silent.

They looked miserable.

"Now watch this" said Dad, "I'll show you coffee's greatest superpower of all."

Ted watched as his Dad walked over to the sad looking group. He heard him order a coffee for each of them. Dad could barely hide his excitement as he skipped around them, waiting for the coffee to arrive. The customers looked at him as though he was some kind of dangerous animal. They didn't want to get too close.

The coffees arrived.

Each person at the table took a sip and suddenly something remarkable and incredible happened. The corners of their mouths all started to twitch. Then they began to grin. Within another twenty seconds they were smiling and another 20 seconds after that they were all beaming with joy.

Dad walked back to Ted, with a smile of his own.

"You see Ted, coffee's greatest superpower - the one that is better then everything else and a truly marvellous gift to the world - is that it brings people together and makes them smile.

Isn't that absolutely wonderful?"

Ted nodded. "Thanks for telling me all about where coffee comes from. But you know, all I really wanted to know is how to get more coffee in my cup."

He tipped his coffee cup upside down. "I've finished."

Dad raised his eyebrows. "So that is all you ever wanted to know from the start?"

He laughed. "Well, that's easy. Excuse me, waiter. Please may we see the coffee menu?"

And Dad and Ted sang...

> *Coffee beans are tough, made of special stuff*
> *Changing shape and size, right before*
> *   our eyes*
> *Drying in the sun, baking till they're done*
> *Roasting all the beans, using big machines*
> *Now we grind and brew, that's the thing*
> *   to do*
> *In a little while, you will start to smile!*
>
> *Superheroes, beans of might*
> *Amazing, awesome, they're alright!"*

MEET SOME OF THE CHILDREN FROM KOROGOCHO!

Your purchase of this book will help to keep their school open and enable them to continue their education.

ABOUT THE AUTHOR

Superhero Coffe Beans! has been written by Emma Dredge, on behalf of In2Ed Africa.

In2Ed Africa works with low-income communities in Eastern Central Africa to provide access to quality education, so that every child has the opportunity to reach their individual potential.

We are committed to transforming global landscapes through our schools and have a real respect for conservation and sustainability, so that communities develop and become self-reliant. Our transformation occurs across many corners of the globe as we bridge the divides of resource rich and resource poor, teaching people that kindness and compassion are priceless.

Inspire: Facebook: fb.me/In2EdAfrica
Collaborate: Instagram @In2Ed_Africa
Educate: www.in2edafrica.org

* * *

To learn more about Emma Dredge and discover more Next Chapter authors, visit our website at www.nextchapter.pub.

Superhero Coffee Beans!
ISBN: 978-4-82417-086-6

Published by
Next Chapter
2-5-6 SANNO
SANNO BRIDGE
143-0023 Ota-Ku, Tokyo
+818035793528

3rd March 2023